PENGUINS ARE AWESOME

by Samantha S. Bell

12 STORY LIBRARY

www.12StoryLibrary.com

12 Story Library is an imprint of Bookstaves and Press Room Editions

Produced for 12 Story Library by Red Line Editorial.

Photographs ©: Volodymyr Goinyk/Shutterstock Images, cover, 1; Ronsmith/Shutterstock Images, 4; Tom K Photo/Shutterstock Images, 5; Libor Fousek/Shutterstock Images, 6; Leona Kali/Shutterstock Images, 7; Evgeny Kovalev spb/Shutterstock Images, 8; Marshall Bruce/iStockphoto, 9; Silvia Pascual/Shutterstock Images, 10; Achim Baque/Shutterstock Images, 11; Josh Anon/Shutterstock Images, 12; sichkarenko.com/Shutterstock Images, 13; jo Crebbin/Shutterstock Images, 14; AndreAnita/Shutterstock Images, 15; JeremyRichards/Shutterstock Images, 16; MalcolmC/Shutterstock Images, 17; prochasson frederic/Shutterstock Images, 18, 28; Sergey Uryadnikov/Shutterstock Images, 19; enchanted_fairy/Shutterstock Images, 20; fieldwork/Shutterstock Images, 21; Roger Clark ARPS/Shutterstock Images, 22; StanislavBeloglazov/Shutterstock Images, 23; niall dunne/Shutterstock Images, 24; vladsilver/Shutterstock Images, 25, 29; Natalia Khalaman/Shutterstock Images, 26; MyImages - Micha/Shutterstock Images, 27

Library of Congress Cataloging-in-Publication Data

Names: Bell, Samantha, author.

Title: Penguins are awesome / by Samantha S. Bell.

Description: Mankato, MN : 12 Story Library, [2018] | Series: Animals are awesome | Audience: Grades 4 to 6. | Includes bibliographical references and index.

Identifiers: LCCN 2016047150 (print) | LCCN 2017002815 (ebook) | ISBN 9781632354365 (hardcover : alk. paper) | ISBN 9781632355041 (pbk. : alk. paper) | ISBN 9781621435563 (hosted e-book)

Subjects: LCSH: Penguins--Miscellanea--Juvenile literature.

Classification: LCC QL696.S47 B45 2018 (print) | LCC QL696.S47 (ebook) | DDC 598.47--dc23

LC record available at https://lccn.loc.gov/2016047150

Printed in China

022017

Access free, up-to-date content on this topic plus a full digital version of this book. Scan the QR code on page 31 or use your school's login at 12StoryLibrary.com.

Table of Contents

1 Penguins Can Be Very Big or Small

Some penguins waddle and hop over rocky ground. Others scoot and slide across the ice. All penguins paddle and glide through the water. With flippers for wings, penguins are birds built for swimming. Some spend 75 percent of their lives in the water.

Most scientists think there are between 17 and 20 different types of penguins. The smallest are little blue penguins, also called fairy penguins. They stand approximately 16 inches (41 cm) tall. They weigh just two to three pounds (0.9 to 1.4 kg).

Emperor penguins are the largest of all penguins. They grow to approximately 45 inches (114 cm) tall. This is the size of an average six-year-old boy. But they are quite heavy. They can weigh 88 pounds (40 kg). This is as much as an average twelve-year-old boy. King penguins are close behind in height. They stand 37 inches (94 cm) tall, but they weigh only 29 pounds (13 kg).

Other species include the macaroni, erect-crested,

Penguins look as though they take flight as they leap into the water from the ice.

King penguins are the second-largest penguin species.

rockhopper, and royal penguins. These penguins all have red beaks and yellow or orange feathers above their eyes. African, Magellanic, and Humboldt penguins have markings on their necks and sides. Little blue penguins have blue-gray feathers. But with their white bellies, all penguins look as if they are wearing tuxedos.

THE WATER KING

In 2007, scientists discovered the first penguin fossil with feathers. Found in Peru, the penguin was named the water king. It stood five feet (152 cm) tall, taller than any penguins alive today. Several of the feathers were reddish-brown or gray. Some scientists believe this means penguins were more colorful long ago.

18

Average number of years penguins live in the wild.

- Penguins are birds that swim instead of fly.
- There are 17 to 20 species of penguins.
- The little blue penguin is the smallest.
- Emperor and king penguins are the largest.

2 Some Penguins Live at the Beach

When people think about a penguin's habitat, many imagine a cold, frozen place. All penguins live south of the equator, but just a few migrate close to the ice and snow of Antarctica. Only emperor and Adélie penguins live there all the time. Emperor penguins survive in temperatures as low as minus-76 degrees Fahrenheit (–60°C).

The rest of the penguin species live in more mild areas. They are found on the rocky shores and sandy beaches of South America, South Africa, and Australia. Nine species breed in the New Zealand region. Galapagos penguins have

Little blue penguins live mainly in Australia. They can also be found in New Zealand, Chile, and Tasmania.

HUMANS WELCOME

With the coldest continent as their home, it is no surprise the penguins in Antarctica do not see many people. They also do not have natural land predators. So when scientists study these penguins, the birds do not seem to mind. The scientists can actually walk right up to them.

2

Number of penguin species that live in the Antarctic.

- All penguins live south of the equator.
- Penguins can be found on ice, beaches, and rocky shores.
- Penguins live as far north as the Galapagos Islands.
- Penguins live in areas where they can find plenty of food.

the warmest homes. They live on the Galapagos Islands near the equator, where temperatures range from 74 to 88 degrees Fahrenheit (23 to 31°C).

No matter what the climate, penguins live where they can find plenty of food. Most live on islands or in remote places where there are not many natural land predators. Otherwise, penguins would always be in danger because they cannot fly.

The Galapagos penguin is only found on the Galapagos Islands.

3

Penguins Use Camouflage

Penguins must watch out for predators. Some come from the air. In the Antarctic, large seabirds called skuas often attack penguin eggs or chicks. Warmer areas may have land predators. Most of them have been brought into the area by humans. They include cats, dogs, and pigs.

Some of the biggest natural threats to penguins come from the water. Leopard seals hide under ice floes. They try to attack penguins as the birds swim back to shore. Sea lions and orcas also try to catch penguins.

Penguins have camouflage to help them hide from predators.

A southern polar skua (left) and an Antarctic penguin

A leopard seal waits in the water for gentoo penguins to jump in.

When predators look down on the ocean surface, the water appears dark. A penguin's black back makes it hard to see from above. When a predator looks up from below the water's surface, the ocean appears lighter in color. So a penguin's white belly helps camouflage it from predators swimming underneath it. Penguins' white bellies also help them sneak up on fish they are hunting.

10

Number of known predators of Magellanic penguins.

- In the Antarctic, birds called skuas attack eggs or chicks.
- Land predators include cats, dogs, and pigs.
- In the water, penguins may be attacked by leopard seals, sea lions, or orcas.
- A penguin's black-and-white coloring helps camouflage it in the ocean.

THINK ABOUT IT

Most of a penguin's land predators have been brought in from other places by people. What effect does this have on penguins? Do you think a penguin's black-and-white coloring helps camouflage it on land?

4

Penguins Have Special Tongues

All penguins eat fish, squid, and crustaceans, especially krill. In colder areas, fish often swim near the ocean floor. Penguins in these habitats must dive deep to find food. Emperor penguins can dive 1,800 feet (550 m) deep for more than 20 minutes at a time. In warmer climates, fish swim in huge schools closer to the water's surface. Penguins in these areas can spend only a few minutes underwater.

Even though penguins are carnivores, they do not have teeth to chew their food. Instead, they swallow it whole. Penguins have soft spines on their tongues and inside their mouths. These spines help push the food down their throats.

Humboldt penguins can swim up to 30 miles per hour (48 km/h) to catch small fish and krill.

NIGHT HUNTING

Some chinstrap and macaroni penguins hunt in the dark. They feed on the krill that comes to the ocean's surface at night. The krill are bioluminescent. This means they glow in the dark. This makes it easy for the penguins to find them. King penguins also hunt at night. They look for lantern fish. These deep-sea fish also produce light.

2

Pounds (0.9 kg) of food a medium-sized penguin eats each day.

- Penguins eat fish, squid, and crustaceans they catch while swimming.
- Some penguins dive deep to find food.
- Penguins swallow their food whole.
- Penguins go hunting together.

When penguins hunt, they leave the shore together. Groups of 10 to 20 penguins are common, although some travel in groups of 100 or more. The penguins help each other watch out for predators. Since there are so many penguins in the group, they have less of a chance of being caught. The large group often stays together until it is a few miles away from the dangerous shoreline, where predators may be waiting.

The spines on a penguin's tongue help the bird grip its prey.

5

Penguins Sneeze Salt

Penguins catch and eat their food as they swim. This means penguins take in a lot of salt water while they eat. If people drink salt water, they become dehydrated. But penguins have a way of getting rid of all that extra salt.

When a penguin drinks salt water, the salt goes into its bloodstream. Like other seabirds, penguins have special glands near their eyes. These glands remove the salt. Then a very salty liquid drips down the penguin's beak. It runs out the

A rockhopper penguin drinks from a geyser.

A gentoo penguin drinks water in Antarctica.

penguin's nostrils. The penguin shakes its head, which makes it look as if it is sneezing salt water.

Although penguins can drink seawater, they also drink freshwater. They find freshwater in puddles or streams. Penguins in cold climates will even eat snow.

2

Number of salt glands a penguin has.

- Penguins ingest a lot of salt water when they eat.
- The salt is filtered from the bloodstream by a gland near the eye.
- Penguins sneeze the salt through their bills.
- Penguins get freshwater from puddles, streams, and snow.

TURNING PINK

African penguins have a special gland above each eye. The glands are just below the skin. They help the penguins cope with the hot temperatures in South Africa. As the penguins get hot, more blood goes to the gland. The blood makes the gland look pink. Since the blood is near the surface, it can cool off in the air. The hotter the penguin gets, the pinker the gland appears.

6

Penguins Can See Colors

A penguin's eyes are suited for life both in the water and on land. They can see clearly underwater to find prey. Like other birds, penguins can see in color. But they cannot see red, a color that is not visible underwater. Instead, penguins see blues, greens, and violets.

Penguins are stinky animals. But their bad odor helps them find each other. Humboldt penguins live on the cliffs of Peru. They spend a long time at sea looking for food. When they return, the rest of the colony is packed together on the cliffs. The penguins use their sense of smell to

Rockhopper penguins have red eyes and long yellow eyebrows.

find their mates and other relatives by their scent.

Penguins use special calls to communicate with one another. They make one kind of call when searching for a mate. They make another call to find family members. They make threat calls to defend their territory. Contact calls help a lone penguin find other penguins. Contact calls from emperor and king penguins can be heard 0.5 miles (0.8 km) away.

4

Number of different kinds of calls penguins make.

- Penguins can see clearly both in the air and underwater.
- Penguins use their sense of smell to find family members.
- Some penguins locate their mates by listening for their squawks.
- Penguin calls are made to defend territory or to find other penguins.

King penguins form huge colonies year-round.

7

Penguins Waterproof Their Feathers

Penguins have several types of feathers. Contour feathers are on the outside. They are short and overlap one another to form a protective layer.

Little downy feathers are attached to the contour feathers. Even more downy feathers are attached to the penguin's skin. These feathers provide insulation. Penguins have even tinier feathers that are hard to see without a microscope. When these feathers are out of place, the penguin knows it is time to preen.

A young king penguin with brown downy feathers.

A penguin may spend as many as three hours a day preening and caring for its feathers, both in the water and on land. A gland near the penguin's tail produces a special oil. The penguin spreads the oil across its feathers. The oil helps reduce friction as the penguin swims. It keeps the feathers soft and waterproof. It also helps prevent bacteria and fungi from growing.

Sometimes, penguins preen one another.

THINK ABOUT IT

Penguins have to take care of the feathers on their heads. How do you think they preen these feathers? With the help of a parent or teacher, do some research to see if your answer is correct.

4

Number of different types of feathers a penguin has.

- A penguin's feathers help keep it warm.
- Penguins have a gland that produces waterproofing oil.
- When penguins preen, they spread the oil across their feathers.
- The oil helps the penguins swim faster.

8

Penguins Can Speed through the Air

The shape of a penguin's body helps it move quickly through the water. It is larger in the middle and smaller on both ends. As the penguin swims, the water flows smoothly over its body. A medium-sized penguin can swim four to seven miles per hour (6.4 to 11 km/h). Gentoo penguins are the fastest. They can swim up to 22 miles per hour (35 km/h).

Penguins can move even faster through the air than in the water. This is because there is less resistance in the air. Penguins take

Penguins are excellent swimmers.

advantage of this to give them more speed. They leap out of the water over and over again. This is called porpoising, and it helps the penguins escape from predators.

Penguins are also good at leaping onto the ice. It would take a lot of time to climb onto the ice or a rocky shoreline. Instead, penguins increase their speed and leap out of the water. Emperor penguins can jump approximately 8 to 18 inches (20 to 46 cm) high. Smaller species, such as Adélie penguins, can leap approximately 6 to 10 feet (1.8 to 3 m) high.

5

Speed, in miles per hour (8 km/h), that an Adélie penguin can swim.

- The shape of a penguin's body helps it move easily through the water.
- Gentoo penguins are the fastest swimmers.
- Some penguins porpoise to escape predators.
- Smaller penguins can jump 6 to 10 feet (1.8 to 3 m) into the air.

An African penguin jumps out of the water.

9

Penguin Waste Can Be Seen from Space

Most penguins breed in large colonies. These groups can range from hundreds to thousands of birds. No matter the size of the colony, penguins nest close together. They share information about food sources. They also help one another watch for predators. Only the yellow-eyed and Fiordland crested penguins nest by themselves. Their nests are spaced out or hidden in the forest.

Fiordland crested penguins nest by themselves.

In the Antarctic, the biggest penguin colonies have so many birds in one place that their waste can be seen from space. The penguin waste stains the ice. Satellite pictures show the dark spots on the ice. These spots help scientists keep track of the penguins. Scientists can even tell the types of penguins in the colony based on the color of the waste.

Penguins return to the same colonies year after year. But some penguins must travel a long way to get there. Gentoo penguins on the

Gentoo penguin colonies can be as small as a few dozen members or as large as thousands of members.

Falkland Islands walk approximately two miles (3.2 km). Chinstrap penguins on Deception Island climb hundreds of feet up steep slopes. Many Adélie penguins cross 50 miles (80 km) of sea ice. Some emperor penguins travel 125 miles (201 km).

46

Number of known emperor penguin colonies in Antarctica.

- Most penguin species breed in huge groups.
- Penguins breed in large colonies for protection.
- Penguins return to the same colony each year.
- Scientists can locate some colonies by looking for dark patches of waste.

THINK ABOUT IT

Why do you think some penguins travel so far to nest? With the help of a parent or teacher, find books or websites with information about penguins' long treks.

10

Penguin Parents Take Turns

Penguins make their nests in all kinds of places. Some penguins nest among tree roots or in forests. Others make burrows in the soil. Still others prefer rocky ground. King penguins and emperor penguins do not have nests at all. They use their feet to hold their eggs.

In most species, penguins lay two eggs at a time. Both the mother and father incubate the eggs by taking turns on the nest. While one parent sits on the eggs, the other hunts for food. Penguins that hunt near the shore are usually gone for a day or two. But other species travel tens or hundreds of miles to find food. They may not come back for several weeks. The parent on the nest must wait to eat.

When hatching, penguin chicks chip at the shell until they can push off the top. Sometimes it takes up to three days to get all the way out. Most chicks are covered with white, gray, brown, or black down feathers. These feathers are not waterproof. The chicks cannot swim until they have their contour feathers.

King penguins lay only one egg at a time.

64

Approximate number of days it takes for the egg of an emperor penguin to hatch.

- Penguins build nests in soil, among tree roots, on rocky ground, or on sea ice.
- In most species, penguins lay two eggs.
- Penguins do not eat while sitting on the nest.
- Chicks cannot swim until their contour feathers come in.

PEBBLE PROPOSALS

Adélie and gentoo penguins build their nests with small stones and pebbles. Because they live in the icy Antarctic, rocks can be hard to find. The penguins often fight over rocks or steal them from one another's nests. Sometimes during courtship, males will offer females a pebble as a gift.

A penguin sits on its egg in Australia.

11

Penguins Recognize Each Other's Voices

Both male and female penguin parents feed the chicks. At first, they go into the ocean one at a time to hunt. As the chicks get bigger, the parents both go at the same time. In many species, the chicks come together in large groups called crèches. This keeps them safer from predators.

When the parents return, they regurgitate their food to feed to their chicks. But finding their own chicks among the colony of penguins is not easy. The chicks may move around while they are waiting for their parents to return. Some emperor chicks wander more than one mile (1.6 km) a day. But each chick has a unique call with a certain frequency. The parents can home in on their chick's special frequency. The chick knows the calls of its parents, too.

African penguins typically have two chicks at a time.

Most chicks stay with their parents until they are two to four months old. When the chicks have shed their down and waterproof feathers have come in, it is time for them to be on their own. First, one parent stops feeding them, and then the other stops, too. The chicks move to the edge of the sea and watch the adults dive into the water. Some chicks fall into the water, and others are washed in by a wave. Other chicks may jump into the water. Within a few minutes of being in the water, the chicks figure out how to swim.

8

Age, in weeks, of a little blue penguin when it is ready to live on its own.

- Penguins and their chicks recognize each other's calls.
- They can find each other in a crowded colony.
- Most penguins stay with their parents for two to four months.
- Penguin chicks learn to swim on their own.

Emperor penguin chicks have silver-gray down.

12

Penguins Lose Their Feathers Each Year

Every year at the end of the breeding season, adult penguins go into the ocean for an extreme time of feeding. Some go for a few weeks, while others go for several months. When they finally return, the penguins are the fattest they will be all year. Some may even be twice the size they were before.

It is time for the penguins to molt. Like other birds, penguins have feathers that become worn down and broken. Now new feathers will push the old ones out.

Each year, yellow-eyed penguins molt over three to four weeks in February or March.

Most birds molt throughout the year. But penguins lose all their feathers at one time. This is called a catastrophic molt. Only Galapagos penguins molt more than once per year. Some scientists believe this is because the hot sun at the equator breaks down their feathers faster.

5

Approximate number of weeks most king penguins take to molt.

- Over time, a penguin's feathers will begin to break and wear out.
- The feathers are replaced during the catastrophic molt.
- Penguins cannot swim or fish without feathers.
- They use up fat instead of eating.
- After molting, penguins return to the sea until the next breeding season.

It takes most penguins two to four weeks to regrow all their feathers. Larger species may take four to six weeks to molt. Because penguins cannot swim without feathers, they cannot hunt or eat during this time. Instead, they use energy from the fat they have built up. By the time the molting season is over, some penguins have lost half their weight. But with new feathers, they are ready to return to the sea to hunt.

Fact Sheet

- Penguins spend a lot of time in the water. Some stay in the ocean for as long as five months.
- Some penguins migrate thousands of miles to find food. They can move quickly over ice by sliding, or tobogganing.
- Penguins come ashore to breed, molt, and grow new feathers. They rely on their feathers more than fat to keep them warm.
- The little blue penguin lays the smallest egg. It is two ounces (57 g).

- The emperor penguin lays the largest eggs. They weigh approximately one pound (0.5 kg).
- Some penguins make unique noises. The African penguin makes a sound like a donkey.
- King penguins and emperor penguins lay only one egg at a time. Only the male emperor penguin incubates the egg.

Glossary

bioluminescent
Animals, such as fireflies and deep-sea fish, that give off light.

crustaceans
Water-dwelling animals with an exoskeleton, such as lobsters, shrimp, and crabs.

dehydrated
Having lost water or body fluids.

downy
Soft and fluffy.

floes
Sheets of floating ice.

frequency
The number of sound waves that pass a certain point every second.

incubate
To sit on eggs to hatch them by warmth.

krill
Small shrimp-like crustaceans and their larvae.

regurgitate
To bring back up again.

remote
Far away, distant.

resistance
A slowing force.

For More Information

Books

Marzollo, Jean. *Pierre the Penguin: A True Story*. Ann Arbor, MI: Sleeping Bear Press, 2010.

Rizzo, Johnna. *Oceans: Dolphins, Sharks, Penguins, and More!* Washington, DC: National Geographic Children's Books, 2010.

Simon, Seymour. *Penguins*. New York: HarperCollins, 2009.

Index

About the Author

Samantha S. Bell lives with her family and lots of pets in the foothills of South Carolina. She loves writing about nature, and she is the author or illustrator of more than 60 books for children.